For All the Saints...

For All the Saints...
Praying for the church

by J. E. Eubanks, Jr.

For All the Saints: Praying for the Church

Published by:

Doulos Resources, 195 Mack Edwards Drive, Oakland, TN 38060; PHONE: (901) 451-0356; WEBSITE: www.doulosresources.org.

Please address all questions about rights and reproduction to Doulos Resources, 195 Mack Edwards Drive, Oakland, TN 38060; PHONE: (901) 451-0356; E-MAIL: info@doulosresources.org.

Published 2010

Printed in the United States of America by CreateSpace

ISBN 978-1-449-55749-2

Cover photograph by Tim Nisly, Albuquerque, New Mexico, USA

This booklet is dedicated to the congregation of Hickory Withe Presbyterian Church, beloved saints and fellow laborers for the Kingdom and for Christ's church, and especially to the Women in the Church (WIC) ministry in their faithful efforts to know Christ more deeply and serve Him well.

Table of Contents

Author's Preface

I am humbled by this book.

I recently heard Sinclair Ferguson comment on an event that happened early in his ministry: as an adult in his thirties, he was approached by a major British publisher and asked to write a book on prayer. Ferguson said that in his youth, he was yet just mature enough to respond to that publisher: "I'm far to inexperienced and immature to ably write a book on prayer. Perhaps you should ask a man of more experience and maturity." When he offered suggestions as to whom they might appeal, several times they responded, "we must confess you were not our first choice; we've already asked Mr. *So-and-so*, and he turned us down, saying that he wasn't nearly wise and mature enough to write a book on prayer!"

I empathize with Dr. Ferguson, because I also feel far too inexperienced, immature, and lacking in wisdom to pen an article— much less a book— on the subject of prayer. Indeed, I would not have dared to undertake it, but for the request of my congregation: the women of the congregation I serve asked me to help them find some resources for learning to better pray for the church. I looked and found nothing. They then asked that I might present them with something— anything— to guide them in learning to pray for the church. How could I refuse? So I set out to write a one-page summary, and that became a pamphlet, which grew into a booklet, and eventually a small book.

Not long after I had completed this book, I was asked to lead my presbytery in prayer; it was the second time in less than two years that I had been asked to do so. When I got home, I told Marcie (in a bit of minor panic): "They've asked me to lead in prayer twice, and I've done this book on prayer. What if people get the misimpression that I really do know something about prayer?!?"

I still feel that way; far from an expert on prayer, I feel as though I am only beginning to learn to pray myself. I am a poor example of prayer, and very little of what I know about prayer (which itself is very little) is put into practice.

But I am comforted that there is hope for me yet. And perhaps you, too, might likewise be comforted. Prayer is not beyond our reach, and the simplest and most meager of prayers are taken up by our Savior and perfected, then presented to the Father as righteous intercessions.

The truths presented here, I hope, are not ideas of mine— for that would serve you abysmally. Rather, I trust you will find them to be truths rooted in Scripture, and in the teachings of men far wiser and more experienced than I.

Introduction

"And pray in the Spirit on all occasions with all kinds of prayers and requests. With this in mind, be alert and always keep on praying for all the saints."

–Ephesians 6:18

We must pray. Whether it be in public and in concert with other believers, or privately (perhaps even silently), we pray. Whether it be long and complete, or even as short as, "Oh, God!"– we pray. Even when we lack the words, our hearts and minds offer wordless utterances before the Lord.

And we must pray for the church. While this is not nearly so self-evident as our basic need to pray, it is nevertheless as important. As no Christian has his or her true identity apart from God (therefore we unite ourselves to Him in prayer), so no Christian has his or her true identity as a Christian apart from His Body. St. Augustine said, "He who does not have the church as his mother does not have God as his

Father."[1] Therefore, we both unite ourselves to one another, and to our Savior, in praying for Christ's church.

How do we pray for Christ's church? While there are always particular circumstances in a local congregation, a denomination, or even in the worldwide church that demand specific prayers, there are also some aspects of prayer for the church that we may, and should, always pray for. If we learn to pray for these matters, we will never lack for a subject of prayer. Learning these types of prayers is the focus of this small book.

How do we learn to pray for Christ's church? From the church, of course. And here is our first encouragement: Christ's church spans all the way back to Adam, Eve, and the promise of the Seed of the woman;[2] it includes all of our spiritual ancestors in Old Testament Israel; and continues through the life of Christ and through the New Testament church. It also includes 2000 years— and counting— of church history, and all that history might teach us.

So, we'll begin in Scripture. If our prayers do not have a biblical basis, we must question whether they are worth our time, for they may very well be out of accord with the will of God! Even in wrong prayers,

---

[1] Saint Augustine. Quotes.net, STANDS4 LLC, 2009. http://www.quotes.net/quote/10282, accessed March 4, 2009.

[2] Genesis 3:15 "And I will put enmity between you and the woman, and between your offspring and hers; he will crush your head, and you will strike his heel."

of course, God may change our hearts and draw us nearer to Him and to His will; still, grounding our prayers in Scripture is both helpful and prudent.

On the main, the rest of this book is divided into sections, with each section representing a particular "aspect" of prayer— that is, something in particular that we might pray for the church. In each section, you'll find that there are three parts that follow a few introductory paragraphs; these parts are distinguished in the sections, but it may be helpful if I describe them here:

✦ BIBLICAL BASIS OF PRAYER— the verse(s) that give us the basis for this particular aspect of our prayers, plus a brief explanation of what these verses teach us about prayer.

✦ FOUNDATIONS OF PRAYER— the "big idea" of this aspect of our prayers. What exactly are we praying for when we pray for this aspect of Christ's church? This part of each section has several facets itself: how to pray for your local congregation, how to pray for your congregation's leadership, and how to pray for the universal church.

✦ PRAYER SUMMARY— you may wish to begin regularly praying for the subjects of this book; I hope you do! At the end of each section, I have offered a summary of the more specific parts of each aspect covered in the section, so that you will have a reference for use during prayer.

At the end of the book, there is a brief list of recommended reading. These are books that I have found to be helpful as I have increasingly learned how to pray, and how Scripture urges us as believers to pray. While by no means exhaustive, this list will nevertheless keep even an avid reader occupied.

It is our delight and privilege to come before the Lord in prayer, and I am grateful to God for this opportunity to learn with you how we might pray for Christ's church!

Praying for God's Glory

"One of his disciples said to him, 'Lord, teach us to pray, just as John taught his disciples.'
He said to them, 'When you pray, say: "Father, hallowed be your name..."'"
                                                        –Luke 11:1-2

We are taught by Christ Himself to pray for the glory of God. The word "hallowed" means "greatly revered or respected," and the Greek word in Luke 11:2 means "to sanctify," which is to set apart for a holy purpose.

All of mankind was created for God's glory;[3] we were built to be worshipers, and in our creation God was the object of our worship. In our fallenness, we frequently fail to fulfill this purpose, instead turning frequently to the idols of our hearts— so much so, that the reformer John Calvin commented that,

---

[3] The *Westminster Shorter Catechism* begins with the question, "What is the chief end of man?" and the answer is, "man's chief end is to glorify God and enjoy Him forever."

5

"man's nature, so to speak, is a perpetual factory of idols."[4]

Nevertheless, God's glory is due Him in our worship, both individually and corporately. It is what we were built for; consequently, this is the proper beginning-point for a consideration of how we might pray for the church.

BIBLICAL BASIS

God's glory is a prominent theme throughout the Scriptures, and therefore it ought to be a prominent theme in all of our prayers.[5] The Bible gives us examples of God's leaders (and Jesus Himself) praying: that God would be glorified in the worship and work of individuals and of God's people; that God's glory would be revealed to those who do not believe as a basis for them to come into belief; that the prominence of God's grace and mercy might increase as the world's awareness of His glory increases.

The idolatry of God's people, their tendency toward legalism, and their inclination toward formalism instead of true worship is also a prominent theme throughout the Bible: from the

---

[4] John Calvin, *Institutes of the Christian Religion*, ed. John T. McNeill, trans. Ford Lewis Battles, 2 vols., Library of Christian Classics 20-21 (Philadelphia: Westminster, 1960), 1.11.8.

[5] Psalm 34:3 "Glorify the LORD with me; let us exalt his name together." (CF: Daniel 4:37; John 12:28; John 17:1, 5; Romans 15:5-6.)

golden calves that the Israelites brought from Egypt, to the frequent abandonment of temple worship, to the formalism so frequently checked and challenged by the prophets, to the cleansing of the temple by Jesus, false worship and giving glory to worldly things is nothing new to Christianity (though it continues to be our constant struggle). It is clear why this must be an area of devoted and fervent prayer.

FOUNDATIONS OF PRAYER

Therefore, among the first things we ought to pray for the church is for God's glory to be prominently displayed through the church. God's people are, first and foremost, worshipers— we are called and established by Him to bring glory to Him through our worship, both individually and corporately. Toward that end, God's church is called four things in the Scriptures:

His Body: if we, the church, are the very embodiment of God in this world, then we ought to reflect Him mostly, and ourselves very little. As John the Baptist said, "He must become greater; I must become less."[6] We, also, must become less.

His Family: families have a tendency to either bring prominence to a family name, or shame. So it is with the church. We must pray that God's family would "conduct [ourselves] in a manner worthy of the gospel

---

[6] John 3:30 "He must become greater; I must become less."

of Christ,"[7] and in so doing live up to the family name.

His Bride: as the Bride of Christ, we are being prepared for His glory: "Let us rejoice and be glad and give him glory! For the wedding of the Lamb has come, and his bride has made herself ready."[8]

His Army: an army protects the honor and integrity of that which it defends. We are to "put aside the deeds of darkness and put on the armor of light"[9] so that we, the church, might bring glory to God.

We should pray that God would exalt His church in the ways that she reflects His glory, and humble her in the ways that she glorifies herself instead of Him. Locally, (this may mean that He allow certain efforts or activities of a church to fade away, if they no longer serve the purposes of advancing God's glory.) It certainly means that His name would be praised and proclaimed boldly in times of

---

[7] Philippians 1:27 "Whatever happens, conduct yourselves in a manner worthy of the gospel of Christ. Then, whether I come and see you or only hear about you in my absence, I will know that you stand firm in one spirit, contending as one man for the faith of the gospel"

[8] Revelation 19:7 "Let us rejoice and be glad and give him glory! For the wedding of the Lamb has come, and his bride has made herself ready."

[9] Romans 13:12 "The night is nearly over; the day is almost here. So let us put aside the deeds of darkness and put on the armor of light."

corporate worship. It may also mean that the ministries of the church might be kept and held loosely by the members, allowing for change and growth as God perfects the efforts of His people, and as they decrease and He increases.

On a broader scale, praying for God's glory in His church may lead us to pray for the efforts of church planting and revitalization by presbyteries, denominations, and other bodies, so that God's Kingdom would continue to advance His glory and truth. Or it might require that we pray for those portions of the church to decline that have turned aside from His glory in favor of worldliness or abandoning orthodoxy.

PRAYER SUMMARY

+ That God's glory would increase, and the glory of man would decrease.

+ That God would sanctify us, His children, in order to bring glory to Himself through His Body.

+ For the preparation of Jesus' Bride for her glorious union with Him at His return, through which His glory would be increasingly evident.

+ That the servants of God would be empowered to bring glory to God, even in the face of opposition.

+ That our hearts would be devoted to God in worship, individually and corporately.

✦ For the glory of the Lord to be clearly displayed before all the world, that the world would see that He is King of kings and Lord of lords.

✦ That the ministries of the Church would bring glory to Him; that those that bring Him glory would prosper, and those that do not would fade away.

✦ For the Kingdom of God to be advanced through an awareness of God's glory, and for the sake of God's glory.

Praying for Unity in the Church

"I have given them the glory that you gave me, that they may be one as we are one: I in them and you in me. May they be brought to complete unity to let the world know that you sent me and have loved them even as you have loved me."
—John 17:22-23

One of the most frequent teachings that Christ offered to His disciples is that they be united together. In fact, Jesus and the apostles make it clear that the primary way that the world will know that the Gospel of Christ is true will be through our unity and love for one another.[10]

The division, lack of acceptance, and unloving spirit that dominates the church today flies in the face of this— it should not be difficult to understand why so much of the world has easily dismissed the church's message as irrelevant and suspect. We should therefore make praying for the unity of the church one of our most frequent concerns in prayer.

---

[10] See also the section on "Praying for the Fellowship of the Saints" for more on this topic.

BIBLICAL BASIS

Scripture frequently shows us pictures of unity in the face of diversity and even disagreement. Old Testament Israel was itself a unity of diversity, with 12 distinct families (though all distant cousins) bound together in one nation. As Jesus gathered His 12 disciples— who would become His apostles— He called men who would be hated enemies in any other context to unite.[11] Even as these apostles disagreed during the establishment of the early church, they sought loving, gracious unity with one another rather than divide.

Since then, the church of Christ has increasingly displayed disunity and brokenness to the world. After centuries of a united, single world church came the division of the church into eastern and western, then increasing division in Europe. By the time of the settling of the Americas, the divided church was the norm. Today, we casually accept the fact of thousands of protestant denominations, often separated for petty or even forgotten reasons.

---

[11] Matthew 10:2-4 "These are the names of the twelve apostles: first, Simon (who is called Peter) and his brother Andrew; James son of Zebedee, and his brother John; Philip and Bartholomew; Thomas and Matthew the tax collector; James son of Alphaeus, and Thaddaeus; Simon the Zealot and Judas Iscariot, who betrayed him." Zealots, such as Simon, were sworn enemies of those who were sympathetic to the Roman powers, such as Matthew the tax collector.

When we pray for unity, we must first look in the mirror: what must I pray for regarding my own failure to strive for unity with my brothers and sisters in Christ? How have I made it difficult for others to feel and be united with me? How ought my union with Christ change my attitude, actions, and heart toward others?

Because of our pride and tendency to accuse, it is often dangerous to pray these same things specifically for others in our local congregation; too often we judge and chastise them in our hearts, regardless of whether our assumptions are well-founded. Therefore, we must be careful when we pray for others about unity; perhaps we might usually pray more generally for them, that Christ would continue to bring growth, humility, and a spirit of unity within them.

As we pray for the church's unity, we might also focus on how we often give undue priority to minor issues, while failing to allow major agreements to be places where we unite. Be it an individual of one tradition rejecting one of another tradition; one local congregation comparing itself to another; or division based on broad theological or denominational boundaries, the history of the church shows we separate more than we unite.

Therefore, we should pray that our hearts, and the hearts of believers everywhere, would be broken about our disunity. We should pray that Christ would give us a capacity for love that would overcome minor distinctions and disagreements. We should pray that He would show us opportunities to unite, and give us the humility and bravery to do so. And that He would protect us from division, and give us a healthy grief for the division that we, and our spiritual ancestors, have glibly participated in.

Finally, we must pray for the leaders of our church to be united, for they will lead us into greater unity or disunity. Pray that they too would overcome the pettiness of minor issues and seek to be bound together more fully rather than distinguished from each other. Pray that even their disagreements would be handled with love and humility, that unity might be preserved. Pray that Christ might use them to minister unity among the whole church, growing us together more and more as His return approaches.

PRAYER SUMMARY

- ✦ For our own hearts to be broken of pride and transformed in Gospel humility and confidence, that we might love our brothers and sisters better.

- ✦ That the Father might minister His grace to our brothers and sisters in Christ, that in Him and through Him we might all grow closer together.

- ✦ Confess that we (the church) have too easily allowed division to define us, rather than the love that Christ urged would define us.

- That He would break our hearts about the division in the church today, and bring about repentance in His church for our tendency to divide; that he would give us a spirit of unity toward one another.

- For Jesus to show us what is of the highest importance: that we are united with Him, and therefore are united with all who are His; that He would give us a greater love and unity with others, even when we have differences or disagreements.

- That God would bring about reunion within His church, allowing us to seek true unity without compromising vital truths; that He would give us discernment about which truths are of major significance and which are of minor importance.

- For Jesus' church to be brought into complete unity so that His truth and glory might be displayed to the world.

Praying for the Proclamation of God's Word

"Preach the Word; be prepared in season and out of season; correct, rebuke and encourage—with great patience and careful instruction."
—II Timothy 4:2

There are three things that the Bible portrays as vital in the life of a church: Word, Sacrament, and discipline. It has been said that any congregation that does not have all three faithfully exercised is not a church![12] Clearly, then, our prayers ought to include these three.

BIBLICAL BASIS

The preaching of God's Word is of vital importance to God's people, and to the church as a whole. Paul emphasizes its significance when he describes how essential preaching is for belief:

> "For there is no difference between Jew and Gentile—the same Lord is Lord of all and richly blesses all who call on him, for,

---

[12] Dr. Donald MacNair, in a lecture on church health.

'Everyone who calls on the name of the Lord will be saved.' How, then, can they call on the one they have not believed in? And how can they believe in the one of whom they have not heard? And how can they hear without someone preaching to them? And how can they preach unless they are sent? As it is written, 'How beautiful are the feet of those who bring good news!'"[13]

He goes on, in other letters, to emphasize preaching even more, when he presents it as the very Word of God Himself: "And we also thank God continually because, when you received the word of God, which you heard from us, you accepted it not as the word of men, but as it actually is, the word of God, which is at work in you who believe."[14] The writer to the Hebrews, also, affirms this view,[15] as does the Apostle Peter.[16]

This biblical teaching is what led John Calvin to conclude that, "When a man has climbed up into the pulpit... it is [so] that God may speak to us by the

---

[13] Romans 10:12-15.

[14] I Thessalonians 2:13.

[15] Hebrews 13:7 "Remember your leaders, who spoke the word of God to you. Consider the outcome of their way of life and imitate their faith."

[16] I Peter 1:23-25 "For you have been born again, not of perishable seed, but of imperishable, through the living and enduring word of God. For, 'All men are like grass, and all their glory is like the flowers of the field; the grass withers and the flowers fall, but the word of the Lord stands forever.' And this is the word that was preached to you."

mouth of a man."[17] In fact, the Reformed confessions and catechisms teach exactly this:

> "The Spirit of God makes the reading, but especially the preaching of the Word, an effectual means of enlightening, convincing, and humbling sinners, of driving them out of themselves, and drawing them to Christ; of conforming them to his image, and subduing them to his will; of strengthening them against temptations and corruptions, of building them up in grace, and establishing their hearts in holiness and comfort through faith unto salvation."[18]

Or, as the Second Helvetic Confession says, the Word of God rightly preached IS the very Word of God.[19]

FOUNDATIONS OF PRAYER

Obviously, then, a Christian ought to be concerned with praying for the preaching of the Word of God, since it is of such vital importance to him or her. Since, through the preaching of the Word then we are brought from unbelief into belief, we ought to pray, like the father of the dying child in the gospel of Mark, "I do believe; help me overcome my unbelief!"[20] Even as we, too, continue in a

---

[17] Sermon XXII on I Tim 3:2 "apt to teach", quoted in THL Parker, *Calvin's Preaching*, Westminster/ John Knox, 1992, p.24.

[18] Westminster Larger Catechism, question #155.

[19] Second Helvetic Confession, I.4.

[20] Mark 9:24.

mixture of belief and unbelief, the preaching of the Word draws us ever nearer to God in belief.

We ought also to pray that the preaching of the Word in our congregation— and, indeed, in all congregations— would be a faithful exposition of all of Scripture. It is too easy for a pastor to focus on a particular area or topic of interest, or to linger in certain books while neglecting others. The predominance of shorter-termed ministries, often lasting only a handful of years, can contribute to this: a pastor who is only among a congregation for a few years does not have time to move from one portion of Scripture to another, yet his successor might only attend to the same general sections. Pray that preachers in all churches, and especially yours, would preach the whole counsel of God.

We might also pray for the protection of the preaching of the Word itself. Too many times, I have heard a sermon that purported to be an exposition of God's Word— it even began with a reading of a lengthy passage— and yet the preaching that followed had little to do with what that text actually said. Instead it served as a launch-pad into the preacher's favorite topic, or worse: it became the basis for moralism or legalism. While the Scriptures do, indeed, teach us the law of God, and they do instruct us in a certain kind of morality, these are not the essential and central message of the Bible. The central message of the Bible is the cross; it is how sinners might be reconciled to God. Pray for the protection of the preaching at your church, in your denomination, and in the church universal, that the central message of the Bible might always be proclaimed boldly, to the converted and unconverted alike.

From there, we ought to pray for the preaching of the Word of God in three ways:

Preparation. Someone will be preaching; we should pray for his preparation: for his study, for discernment, for submission to the illumination of the Holy Spirit, for confidence and boldness. Likewise, someone will be listening; we should pray for their preparation as well: that their hearts will be softened and prepared, that their eyes would be opened and ears unstopped to the truth of Scripture, that they would be made ready by the Holy Spirit in every way.

Delivery. Here again, pray for the preacher to have boldness and confidence in delivering God's Word, for him to have good recall of what he must say, and for him to be faithful to what God would have him speak. Pray also for "unction"— that particular anointing of the Holy Spirit that allows and enables a preacher to effectively deliver the message of God to His people. And pray for the listeners — that they may be attentive, and freed from distraction; that they would be well-prepared to hear, learn, and grow; and that the Holy

Spirit would work in their hearts and minds to urge, encourage, rebuke, and train them.

Response. There is always a response to the Word of God preached. Pray for the preacher to be protected from Satan, the Accuser of the his heart, who will try to persuade him that his preaching had no effect, or that it drove people away from Christ instead of to Him! Pray for the listeners, that the preached Word would linger in their ears and continue to remind them of the truths of God, and that they would receive and understand these truths for the strengthening of their faith.

When we pray for each of these, we might pray for both our local congregation (how might each of these be fulfilled among us?) and for other congregations and even denominations. More and more churches are turning aside from the faithful preaching of God's Word, making sermons ever-shorter and less-full of truth. Whether it be because of inappropriate over-emphasis on music or other aspects of worship, a desire to get out of worship sooner, or simply a low view of preaching (or of the Word as a whole), we ought to pray that all congregations— including our own— would repent of their tendency to neglect God's Word and attend more faithfully to its preaching.

✦ For God to be at work in the faithful preaching of His Word in the church, instructing the saints in the truths He would have us to know and believe.

✦ That the Father would attend to the man who will preach at your church this week, encouraging and instructing him as he prepares to deliver God's Word to God's people; that He would give him diligence, understanding, and wisdom in his studies.

✦ For Christ to prepare His people to hear the Word as it is preached; for Him to open eyes, unstop ears, soften hearts, and make minds attentive to His truth.

✦ That the Holy Spirit would be present during the preaching of the Word; that He would make His presence known through the empowerment that He gives to the preacher, and through revealing truth to all who are listening.

✦ Thanksgiving for the pastor who has labored on behalf of your congregation to deliver God's Word to you; that God would protect his heart from his own second-guessing, as well as from Satan's attacks, and give him confidence in the Spirit-borne fruit of his labors.

✦ Confess how easy it is to be indifferent to the truths heard in a sermon, even in the moments during and immediately following it.

✦ Pray that God would help you to not only hear His Word preached, but to hide it in your heart and learn from it as you grow in your faith.

✦ That those who have grown cold toward preaching would be brought to grief of their sin, and that they would be urged by the Holy Spirit to increase in desire and appreciation for the preaching of God's Word.

Praying for the Administration of the Sacraments

"While they were eating, Jesus took bread, gave thanks and broke it, and gave it to his disciples, saying, 'Take and eat; this is my body.' Then he took the cup, gave thanks and offered it to them, saying, 'Drink from it, all of you. This is my blood of the covenant, which is poured out for many for the forgiveness of sins.'"

–Matthew 26:26-28

The Sacraments of Baptism and the Lord's Supper are means of God's grace— instruments through which God conveys His grace to us, reminds us of His work on our behalf, and seals us unto Himself in a covenantal manner. They were instituted by Christ Himself, and in so doing He gave them to us as Sacraments. They, along with prayer and the preaching of the Word, are the primary means of grace by which we know and receive God's grace as a community of faith.

BIBLICAL BASIS

The administration of the Sacraments is a vital part of church life— as important as preaching and prayer. The apostle Paul said of the Lord's Supper that, "whenever you eat this bread and drink this cup, you proclaim the Lord's death until he comes"[21] — suggesting that, in the absence of Communion rightly celebrated, the proclamation of the cross is weakened. In Acts, Luke portrays the regular (daily?) life of the church included fellowship, hearing "the apostles' teaching" (which would have been the preaching of the Word), the sharing of the Sacrament of the Lord's Supper, and prayer.[22]

FOUNDATIONS OF PRAYER

When we pray for the administration of the Sacraments, then, we might well begin with praying that we will value them as Christ and the apostles valued them— which was not a little. We should pray that our local congregation would take them seriously, and see them as the blessings that they are as means of grace. And we might pray that the grace that they confer would be strength and encouragement to the church universal, and that in "proclaiming the Lord's death until He comes," unbelievers might come to faith.

As important as the Sacraments are, a number of difficulties often arise in churches concerning them that also could be matters of prayer:

They are given too much meaning: though the Sacraments are means of grace, they do

---

[21] I Corinthians 11:26.

[22] Acts 2:42 "They devoted themselves to the apostles' teaching and to the fellowship, to the breaking of bread and to prayer."

not save, nor are they *required* for salvation. To add the requirement of participation in a sacramental act for salvation would render our salvation as due to a work on our part, which is contrary to Scripture.

They are given too little meaning: Some congregations (and denominations) undervalue the Sacraments by reducing their meaning— and therefore their importance— to something less than what Scripture teaches, rendering them as flourishes of memorial significance, at best.

They become routine: frequent and regular practice of the Sacraments might lead congregants to find them dull. Anything that is a regular part of worship can fall victim to this— the preaching of the Word is a perfect example. When this happens to the Sacraments, it is not the fault of the frequency or the regularity, but of the worshiper.

They become neglected: at the other end of the spectrum, some value the Sacraments theoretically, but they practice them so infrequently (fearing routine, perhaps) that the meaning is obscured or implicitly undermined.

They are too easy: the Sacraments are given for the church— not for just anyone. Not guarding them sufficiently can, and will, allow some to partake of them who ought not, and in so doing bring judgment on themselves.[23]

They are too hard: again, we sometimes tend flee to the other end of the spectrum. In effort to guard them, we must be careful that we do not set the bar so high that we exclude those whom we ought to include.

In praying for any or all of the above, consider whether they are true of your participation in the Sacraments; whether they are true of your congregation in general; and whether they are true of the denomination your congregation is a member of. Pray that the Lord would bring your heart and mind into conformity with His Word in the manner in which you view the Sacraments, and pray the same for your congregation and denomination. Pray that He would free you to celebrate the Sacraments with delight and joy, and that He would teach your soul of the grace that they confer to you.

PRAYER SUMMARY

✦ That our gracious God would give His church a deeper and richer appreciation for

---

[23] I Corinthians 11:27-29 "Therefore, whoever eats the bread or drinks the cup of the Lord in an unworthy manner will be guilty of sinning against the body and blood of the Lord. A man ought to examine himself before he eats of the bread and drinks of the cup. For anyone who eats and drinks without recognizing the body of the Lord eats and drinks judgment on himself."

the value of the sacraments, and that we would understand them properly as means of grace.

- ✦ For your congregation's practices of the sacraments to be a vital and vibrant part of body life, and for the body to be strengthened and encouraged by them.

- ✦ That the Lord would protect His means of grace from having too little meaning and importance, and that He would keep His people from importing meanings onto them that He never intended.

- ✦ For the frequency of the practice of the sacraments to be right in your congregation— that they not be neglected, nor that they become routine.

- ✦ That those who are offered the sacraments would understand the importance of the context of the church— that they would not casually approach the sacraments as if they were for just anyone; likewise, that their invitation would welcome them, under the certainty of their profession of faith, without further qualification or obstacle.

- ✦ For all congregations, in celebration of the sacraments, to do so with joy and delight, and for the souls of those who participate to be renewed and taught of the grace of Christ found within them.

Praying for Biblical Discipline & Restoration

"If your brother sins against you, go and show him his fault, just between the two of you. If he listens to you, you have won your brother over. But if he will not listen, take one or two others along, so that 'every matter may be established by the testimony of two or three witnesses.' If he refuses to listen to them, tell it to the church; and if he refuses to listen even to the church, treat him as you would a pagan or a tax collector."

–Matthew 18:15-17

Though sometimes less understood, and frequently less visible, the practice of biblical church discipline is a vital part of church life, together with the preaching of the Word and the administration of the Sacraments. These three together— Word, Sacrament, and discipline— are often referred to as the "marks" of the church, as they denote a congregation or denomination whose life is ordered by the Scriptures themselves.

BIBLICAL BASIS

Throughout the Scriptures, God's people are chastened and disciplined by Him; often, He ordains to use His children to bring about this chastening on individuals within His family. In II Samuel, we read of the prophet Nathan rebuking king David for his sins surrounding Bathsheba, Uriah, and their relationships to David. [24]   Frequently in the New Testament we read of one believer confronting another for their sin, such as Paul addressing Peter for requiring circumcision at conversion.[25]

In the gospel of Matthew, Jesus instructed His disciples in how they ought to deal with matters of correction, when someone had sinned against them: go to him, go again with others if he is unrepentant, go again with the congregation if he still remains

---

[24] II Samuel 12:7-10 "Then Nathan said to David, 'You are the man! This is what the LORD, the God of Israel, says: "I anointed you king over Israel, and I delivered you from the hand of Saul. I gave your master's house to you, and your master's wives into your arms. I gave you the house of Israel and Judah. And if all this had been too little, I would have given you even more. Why did you despise the word of the LORD by doing what is evil in his eyes? You struck down Uriah the Hittite with the sword and took his wife to be your own. You killed him with the sword of the Ammonites. Now, therefore, the sword will never depart from your house, because you despised me and took the wife of Uriah the Hittite to be your own."'" (See all vv.1-14.)

[25] Galatians 2:11-12 "When Peter came to Antioch, I opposed him to his face, because he was clearly in the wrong. Before certain men came from James, he used to eat with the Gentiles. But when they arrived, he began to draw back and separate himself from the Gentiles because he was afraid of those who belonged to the circumcision group."

unrepentant.[26] Today, we follow this pattern as a process for biblical church discipline and restoration.

How is this a pattern for restoration? In every way: if, at any point, the offending brother repents, then he is to be restored. And even if he remains unrepentant, how is he to be treated? As a pagan or a tax collector; and do not forget how Jesus Himself treated pagans and tax collectors, and how He commanded us to treat them: with love, mercy, and kindness, that they may know that the gospel is true.

FOUNDATIONS OF PRAYER

Thus, biblical discipline always has the goal of restoration, or at least of eventual conversion (which could be described, perhaps, simply as restoration on a much grander scale). And this is where we must begin as we pray: that those who have sinned and been sinned against would be restored and reconciled. Whether the steps being taken by one believer toward another are in the earliest and least formalized stages, or whether they are advanced and approaching excommunication, we must pray at all

---

[26] Matthew 18:15-17 "If your brother sins against you, go and show him his fault, just between the two of you. If he listens to you, you have won your brother over. But if he will not listen, take one or two others along, so that 'every matter may be established by the testimony of two or three witnesses.' If he refuses to listen to them, tell it to the church; and if he refuses to listen even to the church, treat him as you would a pagan or a tax collector."

times for the restoration of the sinning church member.

We ought to also pray for patience and perseverance through the process of discipline and restoration. It can be, and often is, a difficult process; it is filled with awkwardness, defensiveness, misunderstanding, and pride. It is a process whose value is sometimes obscured until the process is concluded, and it is far too easy to abandon it. Therefore, pray that all who are involved would be patient in waiting for repentance, and that they would persevere during the difficulties of the process.

Of course, all of this presupposes that a congregation— and the members of that congregation— are actually practicing biblical discipline toward restoration. Sometimes we do not; we fear confrontation too much, and are convinced that such a pattern will yield further division rather than reconciliation. Therefore, we must pray for our souls, that we would see that God would not instruct us to interact in a manner that He would not bless with fruitful response; and we must pray that we would find the bravery and boldness to lovingly address sin where it is committed in accordance with His instructions.

At other times we do not practice biblical discipline because we have too low a view of sin. We don't consider our sin— or the sin of others against us— worth attending to, or we don't regard the breaking of relationships among God's people as substantial. The result of such a view is both the cheapening of Christ's work on the cross and the establishment of an environment where no one is free to struggle with the realities of sin and brokenness. The children of God feel isolated, alone, and forced to wear a mask of happiness or erect a façade of perfection. Hence, we must pray that the Lord would give us an ever-increasing awareness of the severity of our sin; an even greater understanding of the substance of the cross; and the honesty and vulnerability to deal with sin— ours and others'— with love, grace, and repentance.

Still other times, we do not practice biblical discipline *toward restoration*. We will discipline, sure enough— but the practices of our congregation are so legalistic, so cold, so unloving that the result is nearly always estrangement. Even in those cases where repentance is achieved, the relationships of one brother to another are damaged beyond repair. In these times, we must pray that we would come into knowledge of God's love so deeply that they would be convicted of our callous spirits; that in effect God would take our hearts of stone and replace them with hearts of flesh.[27]

Finally, we ought to pray for the leadership of our congregation— and of all congregations— to exercise discernment, wisdom, and prudence in

---

[27] Ezekiel 11:19 "I will give them an undivided heart and put a new spirit in them; I will remove from them their heart of stone and give them a heart of flesh."

leading the congregation through times of discipline and restoration. While God can and does bring glory to Himself and esteem to His church through the discipline process, leading a congregation through it is hard and even costly, as a substantial amount of spiritual and emotional energy is invested. Leaders need patience, that they do not rush to conclusions that God has not yet brought them to; they need grace and forgiveness for those who respond harshly; and they need love above all else. We would do very well to pray for these on their behalf.

PRAYER SUMMARY

+ That the Lord would give to all of His church the hope and goal of true restoration, and that all action of discipline within the church would be conducted in grace, love, and hope.

+ For Christ to grant patience and perseverance to those in His church, especially the leadership, regarding discipline and restoration— that we would wait for the Lord's work, even as He waits patiently for us as well.

+ That your congregation— and all congregations— would be committed and diligent about the practice and pursuit of biblical discipline and restoration.

+ That God would give us an appropriate view of the devastating nature of our sin, and that our hearts would be grieved for sin and for our fallen condition; and that He would consequently motivate us toward practicing biblical discipline and restoration.

✦ That the Lord Jesus Christ would protect our hearts from legalism, from cold indifference, and from an absence of loving hope in our efforts for discipline, and that God would soften our hearts toward others, even in their sinfulness.

✦ For the leadership of our congregations, as they serve, lead, and model humility, godliness, patience, and love throughout the process of discipline and restoration— for God to continue to work in and through them to accomplish His purposes, even that of restoring the one into the 99.

Praying for Repentance & Forgiveness

"Then Peter came to Jesus and asked, 'Lord, how many times shall I forgive my brother when he sins against me? Up to seven times?' Jesus answered, 'I tell you, not seven times, but seventy-seven times.'"
—Matthew 18:21-22

The Bible doesn't simply teach us to pursue repentance from one another; it also requires that we extend forgiveness when we have been sinned against, as Matthew records even just a few verses after Jesus' instructions about discipline and restoration. We are to forgive just as we ourselves have been forgiven by our Heavenly Father— which is to say, unconditionally and without limit.[28] In fact, Jesus teaches us that our forgiveness will be like unto the manner with which we have forgiven others.[29]

---

[28] Luke 11:4 "Forgive us our sins, for we also forgive everyone who sins against us. And lead us not into temptation."

[29] Matthew 18:35 "This is how my heavenly Father will treat each of you unless you forgive your brother from your heart." (See Matthew 18:23-35; also Matthew 6:14-15; Mark 11:25.)

BIBLICAL BASIS

Beyond this, the Word teaches that we are to proactively offer repentance when we have sinned against others.[30] So if we have been sinned against, we should go to the offender and ask for repentance. But if we have sinned against another, we should go to them and offer repentance. Regardless of where our involvement is, if there is sin then Scripture teaches us that we must actively pursue reconciliation about it.

The purpose of this is several-fold. In humility, we learn our greater dependence on Christ and the cross. Our fellowship is preserved, and we are able to live honestly and vulnerably before one another. This allows for the church to be unified, so that the onlooking world would know that the gospel is true. And all of it brings glory to God.

The nature of repentance is peculiar, as it is clearly something that involves us, yet it is also clear that repentance is not something that we can muster within ourselves or cause ourselves to experience. It, like all of salvation, is an act of God's grace, granting us something that we neither have in ourselves nor deserve to be given.

---

[30] Matthew 5:23-24 "Therefore, if you are offering your gift at the altar and there remember that your brother has something against you, leave your gift there in front of the altar. First go and be reconciled to your brother; then come and offer your gift."

Not unlike the prayers that we offer for the unity of the church, then, we begin our prayers for repentance and forgiveness with self-reflection. From whom do I need to seek forgiveness and offer my repentant heart? What sins are present in my life about which I am yet unrepentant? Who am I harboring an unforgiving spirit against, that I need to offer true forgiveness?

Also like the section above, when we begin to pray for others about repentance and forgiveness we must be careful to avoid a judgmental spirit toward them. Here again, I would suggest that you try to keep your prayers more general, while still offering heartfelt prayers for them. Perhaps something like, "Father, minister Your grace to my brothers and sisters in Christ, that in You and through You we all might forgive and seek forgiveness earnestly..." or "God, please bring about repentance in Your church..."

There are, perhaps, particular sins present in your local congregation that you are aware of. If they are between other individuals, you ought to pray for them to be forgiving where necessary and for the Lord to bring repentance. You might also pray that God would protect your own heart from a gossiping spirit in your knowledge of others' sins! If such sins are corporate in nature— that is, they involve all or a substantial part of the congregation— you should pray that God would bring conviction of sin and a repentant spirit to all. And you ought to pray for the party/parties sinned against in such a way, that the Lord would be preparing in them a heart of forgiveness.[31]

Pray also for widespread repentance for your denomination, particularly if you recognize that it is, in some way, straying from either a commitment to the truth or a commitment to love— nearly all denominations are wayward in one or the other. Pray that the leaders of your denomination, or leaders of a sister denomination, would be bold enough to confront one another in love about these errors, and that they would respond with forgiveness and repentance.

And pray for your church's leaders to be the biggest repenters and forgivers among your congregation. Leaders who are aware of their own sin, lament it, and seek reconciliation about it are true leaders for the church, serving as the under-shepherds that Christ has appointed them to be. Likewise, leaders who respond to sin with a forgiving spirit encourage repentance in those they lead, thereby driving them to Christ. Pray that your congregation's leaders would live out the gospel in this way.

---

[31] See also the section on "Praying for Revival, Revitalization, & Renewal."

PRAYER SUMMARY

✦ For your gracious God to reveal to your heart those sins for which you need to grieve and repent, and for Him to give to you a spirit of forgiveness for those who have sinned against you.

✦ That Jesus would protect your heart, and the hearts of others, from a judgmental spirit in your prayers for them.

✦ For the particular sins and broken relationships in your congregation that you are aware of, and for God to be at work in those circumstances to bring about conviction, repentance, forgiveness, and reconciliation.

✦ That the Lord would work to bring repentance and grief for sin to entire denominations and across the broader church, that the leaders of the universal church would lovingly and uncompromisingly confront one another toward repentance, forgiveness, and reconciliation.

✦ For the leaders of your congregation, and of sister congregations, to be first among those who confront their own sin, and quickest also to forgive those who have sinned against them.

Praying for Fellowship Among the Saints

*"A new command I give you: Love one another. As
I have loved you, so you must love one another. By
this all men will know that you are my disciples, if
you love one another."*

–John 13:34-35

There is no theme more prominent in Scripture
than the theme of love— and a substantial part of the
body of teachings on love is how the children of God
might love one another.

When we think of "fellowship" within the
church, this must be foremost in our notions of what
it means to share in fellowship among the saints.
Often we regard many types of activities— social
events, meals, parties, essentially anything that
doesn't overtly fit into another category— as
"fellowship"; and indeed any of these may include an
element of true fellowship within them. But biblical
fellowship, while not necessarily other than these, is
necessarily more than them.

Fellowship is in inherently spiritual endeavor,
and takes its cues from nothing less than our

salvation, being justified before God: the function and goal of our reconciliation to God through Christ is that we might be restored to fellowship with Him. Where once we were enemies, now we have the fellowship of being sons and daughters of God, through His love for us.

Fellowship among Christians, therefore, is based on our reconciliation with God and with each other. We cannot share in fellowship with God unless we have been reconciled in Christ; likewise, we cannot share in true fellowship with each other unless we have been reconciled both to God and to one another.[32] And just as our fellowship with God is aimed at deepening our love for Him, so too our fellowship with one another is to be aimed at deepening our love for each other. When Christians think of fellowship, therefore, their minds ought to think of those opportunities and occasions wherein their relationships with each other might be deepened, strengthened, and purified.

BIBLICAL BASIS

The "one another" commands of the New Testament serve the purpose of fleshing this out very well: be devoted to one another; honor one another. Live in harmony with one another. Love one another. Stop passing judgment on one another.

---

[32] I John 1:3 "We proclaim to you what we have seen and heard, so that you also may have fellowship with us. And our fellowship is with the Father and with his Son, Jesus Christ."

Accept one another as Christ accepted you. Greet one another with a holy kiss.[33] Agree with one another.[34] Serve one another in love.[35] Bear with one another in love. Be kind and compassionate to one another. Speak to one another in psalms, hymns, and spiritual songs. Submit to one another.[36] Forgive each other. Teach and admonish one another.[37] Encourage one another.[38] Spur one another on to love and good deeds.[39] Live in harmony with one another. Offer hospitality to one another. Clothe yourselves in humility with one another. Greet one another with love.[40] Love one another.[41]

Relating to each other in love is vital for the health of the church. When we love each other, repentance and forgiveness comes more easily. We suffer fewer distractions in worship, and celebrate the joy of the Sacraments and the restoration of discipline more fervently together. We grow spiritually, as we are better able to encourage one another in our faith. When we suffer and grieve, we do not feel alone. The unconverted, seeing our love

---

[33] Romans 12:10; 12:16; 13:8; 14:13; 15:7; 16:16.

[34] I Corinthians 1:12.

[35] Galatians 5:13.

[36] Ephesians 4:2; 4:32; 5:19; 5:21.

[37] Colossians 3:13; 3:16.

[38] I Thessalonians 5:11; Hebrews 3:13; 10:25.

[39] Hebrews 10:24.

[40] I Peter 3:8; 4:9; 5:5; 5:14.

[41] I John 3:11; 3:23; 4:7; 4:11; 4:12; II John 5.

for each other and the consequent fellowship, become convinced of the truth of the gospel and are converted. God Himself is reflected accurately to believers and unbelievers alike. When we fail to live in fellowship and love, all of these are threatened.

FOUNDATIONS OF PRAYER

We must pray for our love to be developed, that we would be transformed into the image of Christ more fully in the ways of love. All of us are immature in our capacity for love, and even our best love is selfish in nature. We need to learn selflessness and self-denial in our love for one another. Pray that your local congregation might increase in selfless love for each other.

True fellowship born out of love creates a culture of authenticity, honesty, and vulnerability. We are free to be ourselves, and need not hide our struggles or our failures. We love others as they are, and we are loved as we are. We should pray that such a culture would define our congregation, and that we would grow in our love for others even in the difficulty of seeing their sin and struggles, just as they would grow in love for us in spite of our sin.

This kind of fellowship is also an environment of hospitality, and we can pray that God would grant us opportunities to extend hospitality to one another, serving each other in times of contentment and in times of need. We should pray that we would respond to these opportunities with willingness, both to serve and to be served.

Finally, pray that God would protect our love from selfishness, from proud deceit, and from obliging one another by our acts of service. Pray that we would not mistake mere "entertaining" for true hospitality. Pray that we would not get caught up in comparing ourselves to others, nor that our efforts to love and serve would puff us up.

PRAYER SUMMARY

+ For God to strengthen our love for others, and to give us love for those for whom we lack true biblical love; and for Him to mature us in our capacity for loving others, giving us self-denial and hearts of service toward others.

+ That in our loving fellowship we might learn to be honest, vulnerable, and authentic, and that we are accepting of others in their vulnerability, and we in ours.

+ For a spirit of hospitality to permeate our community, and that Christ would make us willing participants in hospitality.

+ That God would protect us from selfishness, pride, and false fellowship.

Praying for Spiritual Growth

"Then we will no longer be infants, tossed back and forth by the waves, and blown here and there by every wind of teaching and by the cunning and craftiness of men in their deceitful scheming. Instead, speaking the truth in love, we will in all things grow up into him who is the Head, that is, Christ. From him the whole body, joined and held together by every supporting ligament, grows and builds itself up in love, as each part does its work."
–Ephesians 4:14-16

Christ longs for us to know Him fully and completely, and that our knowledge would develop and mature. The Scriptures are replete with descriptions of growing in our faith: Peter urges us to "grow in the grace and knowledge of our Lord and Savior Jesus Christ."[42] Paul encourages the Romans that they are "complete in knowledge"[43] and says to the Colossians that, "My purpose is that they may be encouraged in heart and united in love, so that they may have the full riches of complete understanding,

---

[42] II Peter 3:18.

[43] Romans 15:14 "I myself am convinced, my brothers, that you yourselves are full of goodness, complete in knowledge and competent to instruct one another."

in order that they may know the mystery of God, namely, Christ."[44]

BIBLICAL BASIS

One common metaphor in the Bible is the comparison between the spiritual "food" of immature Christians, who (like infants) drink milk, as opposed to those who are mature in their faith and eat meat. Paul uses it when he writes to the Corinthians about their growth in the faith;[45] the writer to the Hebrews does the same.[46] Peter writes: "like newborn babies, crave pure spiritual milk, so that by it you may grow up in your salvation."[47]

In Ephesians 4:14-16, Paul describes what such spiritual maturity looks like:

✦ We are no longer susceptible to being easily persuaded about variations in doctrine. Instead, we have a healthy awareness of wrong teaching, and we can recognize when someone is teaching the Bible improperly or offering us a false doctrine.

---

[44] Colossians 2:2.

[45] I Corinthians 3:2 "For I resolved to know nothing while I was with you except Jesus Christ and him crucified."

[46] Hebrews 5:12-13 "In fact, though by this time you ought to be teachers, you need someone to teach you the elementary truths of God's word all over again. You need milk, not solid food! Anyone who lives on milk, being still an infant, is not acquainted with the teaching about righteousness."

[47] I Peter 2:2.

- We do not follow ungodly or unbiblical leadership. Thus, we are not deceived by their schemes to aspire to power, nor are we tricked into accepting their false teachings.

- We are able to properly balance both truth and love in all that we do. We neither overemphasize truth in a callous or domineering way, nor urge loving one another to the exclusion or reduction of truth. We have learned from Christ how both may be present.

- We have grown, and are growing, in our knowledge of Jesus Christ. We understand His life and work on our behalf, why it was necessary, and how He continues in that work today. And we know what the future holds for us as believers.

- We are united in love and fellowship to the church. We realize that we need the genuine fellowship of the Body of Christ to survive and grow, and don't believe in a "lone ranger" practice of Christianity. Instead, we are actively involved in the life of the church, in worship, fellowship, service, and hospitality.

- We understand our good and proper place of contribution to the church, and delight to fulfill it. We recognize that Christ has uniquely crafted and gifted us for His service in the church and Kingdom, and we are eager to accept the role(s) He has given us. We find fulfillment in this above all else.

FOUNDATIONS OF PRAYER

Understanding this comprehensive view of spiritual growth gives us much to pray for about Christ's church. To begin with, we should pray that we— and all of the fellow believers in our local congregation— understand and prize spiritual growth, and that we might aspire to it. We should pray that God would be about the work of bringing spiritual growth within us and those around us, for it is by His grace that we receive growth.

We might offer very specific prayers in this way: that we would be more diligent in reading the Bible and praying, and in committing ourselves to worship and other congregational activities. That we would grow as readers and learners, taking up some of the many fine books and journals available to us. That God would give us wisdom and discernment about how He has made and formed us, that we might serve Him. That we would increase daily in our love and fellowship with one another.

Likewise, we should pray for our denomination, and for other congregations and denominations, that they would grow and mature spiritually. Biblical illiteracy and spiritual immaturity is more uniformly present in all churches in our day than ever before— no congregation or denomination is immune. Even in those that are growing in size (which is not most congregations or denominations), there is a danger of becoming "a mile wide and an inch deep." Pray that God would grow His church in spiritual depth, as well as numerically.

We ought to also pray for protection. As we grow in knowledge of Christ and in spiritual maturity, it is far too easy for this to puff up our pride, giving us a haughty air and a disdain for those who are less mature. Lord, protect us from ourselves in that way! Yet, we should also pray that He would protect us from rejecting spiritual growth out of fear of such arrogance: some actually teach that we ought not aspire to greater knowledge, simply because knowledge puffs up. We must pray for the balance of truth and love to be always present, even (and perhaps especially) in our demeanor toward others as we grow.

We ought to pray for protection, as well, specifically from those leaders who would exercise "cunning and craftiness of men in their deceitful scheming."[48] Too many have found the church to be a willing playground for their selfish gain, and have plied their con acts upon God's well-meaning people. Today, the teachings of the prosperity "gospel," the "victorious Christian life," and other such heresies are not simply the dangerous waters on the outer

---

[48] Ephesians 4:14 "Then we will no longer be infants, tossed back and forth by the waves, and blown here and there by every wind of teaching and by the cunning and craftiness of men in their deceitful scheming."

borders of the universal church; they have infiltrated even some of the most historically evangelical pulpits and classrooms. In our prayers for maturity for the church, we should include prayers that even the least mature believers would begin to recognize these treacherous con artists for what they are.

Finally, as has become our pattern, we should pray for our leaders about spiritual growth. Immediately before the above passage in Ephesians, Paul gives us insight into *how we grow* spiritually:

> "It was [Christ] who gave some to be apostles, some to be prophets, some to be evangelists, and some to be pastors and teachers, to prepare God's people for works of service, so that the body of Christ may be built up until we all reach unity in the faith and in the knowledge of the Son of God and become mature, attaining to the whole measure of the fullness of Christ.
>
> Then we will no longer be infants..."[49]

Christ has given us pastors, teachers, and other leaders in the church for the purpose of equipping us for spiritual growth. Therefore, we ought to pray for *their* spiritual growth— for seldom is it possible for a congregation to grow more than its leaders. We also should pray for their ability to lead others in spiritual growth, and for their diligent attention to doing so. Pray that they would know how to shepherd us and attend to us, so that they might encourage us toward Christ. And pray that God would protect them from

---

[49] Ephesians 4:11-14a.

error, and give them quick awareness and repentance when they are in error.

PRAYER SUMMARY

+ That God would give us aspiration toward spiritual growth and maturity, as individuals and as a congregation.

+ That the practices of spiritual formation through particular disciplines would be instrumental in bringing true spiritual growth to those in our church.

+ For the Lord's ongoing work in our denomination to bring about spiritual growth and a deepening commitment to it.

+ For protection from pride and fear as we grow, and for a healthy humility in our growth.

+ For Christ to grant continuing spiritual growth and protection for the leaders of our congregation, and for those of our denomination.

Praying for Conversion of the Unconverted

"When the people heard this, they were cut to the heart and said to Peter and the other apostles, 'Brothers, what shall we do?'

Peter replied, 'Repent and be baptized, every one of you, in the name of Jesus Christ for the forgiveness of your sins. And you will receive the gift of the Holy Spirit. The promise is for you and your children and for all who are far off—for all whom the Lord our God will call.'

With many other words he warned them; and he pleaded with them, 'Save yourselves from this corrupt generation.' Those who accepted his message were baptized, and about three thousand were added to their number that day."

—Acts 2:37-41

It should be no secret to a believer that God wants to see others come into saving faith in Him. When Christ commissioned His disciples in their work as apostles, He told them, "go and make disciples of all nations."[50] This wasn't a new idea or command; Abraham was told, "I will make you into a great nation and I will bless you; I will make your name great, and you will be a blessing."[51] Similarly, king David commented that, as a result of God's

---

[50] Matthew 28:19-20 "Therefore go and make disciples of all nations, baptizing them in the name of the Father and of the Son and of the Holy Spirit, and teaching them to obey everything I have commanded you. And surely I am with you always, to the very end of the age."

[51] Genesis 12:2.

work to bring repentance and renewal in David's heart, "Then I will teach transgressors your ways, and sinners will turn back to you."[52]

BIBLICAL BASIS

God's desire for the conversion of sinners is inherent in all that He does throughout the Scriptures. From Genesis 3 onward, until the very fulfillment of the New Jerusalem in Revelation 22, it is plain that, "He is patient with you, not wanting anyone to perish, but everyone to come to repentance."[53]

In His mercy, God has ordained that we, the church, be active in participation of bringing lost souls into conversion. As we have already mentioned, it is especially through the preaching of the Word that God works to teach others of Himself. Through the administration of the Sacraments, the work of the cross is proclaimed and made visible. Our unity as believers is a demonstration to the world that Christ is the Lord, and our love for one another will distinguish us as His disciples. Our spiritual growth will strengthen us and protect us against error, and our use of biblical discipline and restoration will protect us from sin, so that the truth about Christ would not be obscured. And our repentance and forgiveness will demonstrate Christ's love and mercy for us carried out unto one another. In all of these,

---

[52] Psalm 51:13.

[53] II Peter 3:9.

God has used, uses, and will use His church to bring about the conversion of sinners into saints.

FOUNDATIONS OF PRAYER

In effect, then, by praying for all of these (and other aspects of the church in coming sections) we are praying, in part, for the conversion of the unconverted. But we must take our prayers beyond that, and offer specific intercession for the unconverted to know Christ through the church.

We must pray that God's church would be about the work of gathering unbelievers into the church. Too often, believers are caught up in concerns about evangelism— that they won't know what to say, or they are too intimidated, or they are afraid of rejection. Yet God has made it clear that it is not necessarily the work of the individual Christian to evangelize an unbeliever, but the work of His church: the role of the individual Christian is to extend love and hospitality to unbelievers in such a way that they would receive and accept an invitation to hear God's Word preached. A ministry of gathering unbelievers into the church is of primary concern in our prayers. We therefore must pray that God would embolden us, and our fellow believers, in our witness and equip us for the work of evangelism as His church is to be equipped.

We should also pray that the members of our congregation— including ourselves— actually have friendships with unbelievers. Sadly, this is too often the biggest obstacle for Christians wishing to evangelize the lost: they don't actually know any! Pray that the members of your congregation would find delight in meeting and befriending their neighbors, co-workers, and others who they come into contact with.

Pray also for your congregation's hospitality, that when visitors— especially unconverted ones— come into the sanctuary for worship, they would feel a loving welcome from all present. It is already awkward, even foreign, for an unbeliever to come into Christian worship; he or she knows that they don't fit in, that they are outsiders watching from within. As the cross is preached, they may find that their awkwardness turns into offense if their hearts are unprepared for it.[54] Pray that your church would be so hospitable that, even if they were offended by the message of the cross, they are nevertheless compelled to return the next week out of desire to taste of the love and fellowship of the Body again.

Pray likewise for the other congregations in your denomination, and for the worldwide church, that they would have a ministry of gathering and that their preaching of the Word would so consistently point to the cross that no unbeliever could visit

---

[54] I Corinthians 1:23-25 "But we preach Christ crucified: a stumbling block to Jews and foolishness to Gentiles, but to those whom God has called, both Jews and Greeks, Christ the power of God and the wisdom of God. For the foolishness of God is wiser than man's wisdom, and the weakness of God is stronger than man's strength."

without hearing the truth about how they may be saved in Christ. Pray also that they would be places of love and hospitality, demonstrating the love of Christ to the unconverted, and thereby fulfilling Christ's promise that they will know that we are His disciples.

Pray also for the leaders of your congregation to, again, be the first and quickest to live a gathering and hospitable life before the unbelieving world. Pray that they would find opportunity to meet and know unbelievers, particularly since their duties of leadership demand that even more of their time be devoted to the church and to time spent with fellow believers. And pray that they would not be so concerned with their leadership duties that they shirk hospitality, nor that they would be so focused on hospitality as to neglect their responsibilities as leaders.

Finally, pray for those who labor as evangelists and missionaries on behalf of the church to cultures and communities near and far. Pray that they would faithfully proclaim God's Word to all who would listen, in spite of opposition or cultural barrier. Pray that the social and civil structures in place— including laws— would not be a hindrance to their ministry of the truth, and that when they do encounter such obstacles, that they would not be deterred by them. Pray that they would see the fruit of their teaching, and that many would come into belief and be converted; nevertheless, pray that they would remain faithful to their calling regardless of how much or how little fruit they see. And pray that God would use their faithful preaching, teaching, and other labor to carry His Word to every tribe, tongue, and nation, and thereby that He might be glorified and His Kingdom be expanded.

Prayer Summary

+ That you, and the members of your congregation, would diligently gather unbelievers into the church, and boldly speak of the good news of the Gospel to those who do not know Christ.

+ For God to open up to you and others opportunities to befriend and love unbelievers with true neighbor-love.

+ That your congregation would be hospitable to the unconverted, in order that they, as outsiders, might long to be included.

+ For other congregations and for your denomination to frequently and actively gather unbelievers into the church for their souls' sake.

+ That the leaders of your congregation would exercise leadership well in this area.

+ For those whom God has called to serve as evangelists and missionaries to faithfully fulfill their calling, boldly bearing witness to the truth and carrying out fruitful ministry.

Praying for Revival, Revitalization, & Renewal

"You heavens above, rain down righteousness; let the clouds shower it down. Let the earth open wide, let salvation spring up, let righteousness grow with it; I, the LORD, have created it."
–Isaiah 45:8

Revival is a subject that is often talked about in the church, and just as frequently it is misunderstood in its biblical meaning. Many churches host "revivals" on a periodic basis, but these are not (normally) true revivals; a revival is when the Holy Spirit moves widely through a community in such a way as to bring many to repentance at the same time (both among the converted and the unconverted). Historically, true revival has begun, not with a number of outsiders are invited into a special event, but when people within a congregation are brought to renewal through the Gospel. True revival is never the fruit of man's work or plans, but the fruit of God's work.

Dr. Timothy Keller, a prominent Pastor in New York City, said of revival, "When revival breaks out through a recovery of the gospel, three things happen: nominal church members realize they'd never been converted; sleepy, lethargic Christians are energized and renewed; outsider non-Christians are attracted into the beautified worship, community and lives of the converted and renewed church members."[55] When we pray for revival, this is what we must have in view.

Revival alone is not the only goal, however; true revival leads to the revitalization and renewal of the church, locally and more broadly. Many churches exhibit unhealthy symptoms, and need the long-term affects of true revitalization. Dr. Harry Reeder has said, "any church that has been meeting together for more than six months is in need of revitalization in some way."[56]

BIBLICAL BASIS

The need for congregations to be renewed and revitalized is not a new one; the Bible is replete with examples of such congregations.

The "congregation" of Israel is a prime example throughout much of the historical record of the Old Testament. Remember, as a prime example, the

---

[55] Source unknown.

[56] Dr. Harry Reeder is the Senior Pastor of Briarwood Presbyterian Church in Birmingham, AL, and the founder of From Embers to a Flame, a ministry for the revitalization of churches. This comment was made during a From Embers to a Flame conference.

nation-wide revival that took place under the leadership of young king Josiah: setting out to simply rebuild the temple, Josiah's workers came across a copy of the Torah, or "the Book of the Law".[57] It quickly becomes clear to the reader of this passage that none of those involved had ever read it, nor had they heard it read!

As the Book of the Law finds its way to Josiah, he is grieved about the whole situation: "When the king heard the words of the Book of the Law, he tore his robes."[58] Then he inquired of the prophetess Huldah of what the nation must do to return to the Lord,

---

[57] II Kings 22:3-8 "In the eighteenth year of his reign, King Josiah sent the secretary, Shaphan son of Azaliah, the son of Meshullam, to the temple of the LORD. He said: 4 'Go up to Hilkiah the high priest and have him get ready the money that has been brought into the temple of the LORD, which the doorkeepers have collected from the people. Have them entrust it to the men appointed to supervise the work on the temple. And have these men pay the workers who repair the temple of the LORD— the carpenters, the builders and the masons. Also have them purchase timber and dressed stone to repair the temple. But they need not account for the money entrusted to them, because they are acting faithfully.' Hilkiah the high priest said to Shaphan the secretary, 'I have found the Book of the Law in the temple of the LORD.' He gave it to Shaphan, who read it."

[58] II Kings 22:11.

and in response to the word of God in the Torah he led the people of Israel in revival.[59]

Likewise, we find congregations in the New Testament, many of them recently established, in need of revitalization and revival. Having just returned from a missionary journey, the apostle Paul was already concerned for the health of those churches he had helped to establish.[60] His concern was great enough, in fact, that he took Silas with him and set out to revitalize them: "he went through Syria and Cilicia, strengthening the churches."[61]

In fact, the New Testament demonstrates how clearly the need for revitalization and renewal constantly can be. Consider the church in Ephesus: after being established by Paul during his second

---

[59] II Kings 23:1-3 "Then the king called together all the elders of Judah and Jerusalem. He went up to the temple of the LORD with the men of Judah, the people of Jerusalem, the priests and the prophets—all the people from the least to the greatest. He read in their hearing all the words of the Book of the Covenant, which had been found in the temple of the LORD. The king stood by the pillar and renewed the covenant in the presence of the LORD—to follow the LORD and keep his commands, regulations and decrees with all his heart and all his soul, thus confirming the words of the covenant written in this book. Then all the people pledged themselves to the covenant." (Cf. II Kings 23:4ff.)

[60] Acts 15:36 "Some time later Paul said to Barnabas, 'Let us go back and visit the brothers in all the towns where we preached the word of the Lord and see how they are doing.'"

[61] Acts 15:41.

missionary journey,[62] he returns again to be used greatly by the Lord for the growth and establishment of that congregation during his third journey,[63] then follows up with the elders later, warning them of the potential for trouble to come.[64] One would think that, if ever a church were safe from losing sight of the Gospel and becoming unhealthy, the Ephesian church would be it!

Yet we find otherwise through the rest of the New Testament. Paul wrote to them in his epistle to the Ephesians, again reminding them of the truths of the Gospel and urging them to withstand spiritual attack. He wrote again, this time in his letters to Timothy, encouraging his young friend (who was serving as Pastor to the Ephesians) to stand firm for the Gospel and protect the flock from the threat of false teaching. But in spite of Paul's frequent urging and warnings, we still find Christ Himself rebuking them for abandoning the Gospel: "Yet I hold this against you: You have forsaken your first love. Remember the height from which you have fallen! Repent and do the things you did at first. If you do not repent, I will come to you and remove your

---

[62] See Acts 18:19 "They arrived at Ephesus, where Paul left Priscilla and Aquila. He himself went into the synagogue and reasoned with the Jews."

[63] Acts 19:1 "While Apollos was at Corinth, Paul took the road through the interior and arrived at Ephesus." (See also Acts 19:8-20.)

[64] Acts 20:17 "From Miletus, Paul sent to Ephesus for the elders of the church." (See also Acts 20:28-31.)

lampstand from its place."[65] By all evidence, they did not heed this warning; no remnant of Ephesus (the city) exists today, nor does any Ephesian church.

FOUNDATIONS OF PRAYER

If the church in Ephesus was so vulnerable, even with Paul, Timothy, and the revelation of Christ bringing correction to bear, then you can be sure that your congregation is vulnerable, too. We must be vigilant to pray for the health and vitality of our churches, and for true revival and renewal to take place in our midst.

Pray, therefore, that your congregation would not become complacent in the matter of keeping the Gospel central. So many congregations assume that they are healthy, simply because there aren't obvious or major problems in plain view— but the absence of symptoms doesn't preclude real sickness. Pray that your church wouldn't become too comfortable, but would always look for and expect the Gospel to be central.

It may be that your congregation is truly and obviously unhealthy, and the absence of the Gospel is palpable. If your church is in decline because the Gospel is absent, because community-wide sin is present, or both, you must pray for the return of the Gospel. Pray that the Holy Spirit would descend anew on you, and on the whole congregation, and bring renewed repentance and commitment to

---

[65] Revelation 2:4-5.

Christ. Beseech the Lord that the sin that plagues your church would be abandoned, and that He would forgive the congregation of its sin.

Likewise, you should pray for broad-spread repentance among the leadership of your congregation, whether there is corporate sin or not. The Pastor, elders, and other leaders must be the first to return to Gospel hope if they will lead others there too. Pray that they would be quick to acknowledge and grieve their own sin, and eager for the renewal of Christ both personally and corporately. Pray that their humble and frank spirit of repentance would encourage and challenge others in the congregation to also seek a spirit of repentance.

You should also pray for revival in your community, city, state, and country. Pray for revival across your denomination, and across the universal church. Pray that God would expand His kingdom and renew it, granting new vitality to all of the congregations that call themselves His. Pray that He would surprise even the most hopeful and optimistic among us with the bounty of his blessings poured out through true revival across the world.

PRAYER SUMMARY

+ That God would give us an honest awareness of our vulnerability for unhealthy church life, and that He would grant us vigilance in our care and prayerfulness about it.

- For your congregation to keep the Gospel central always, never becoming satisfied that it has been "preached enough".

- That the clear and obvious ways in which your congregation are unhealthy would be revived with vitality and a renewed commitment to Gospel truth.

- For the Lord to make the leadership of your congregation the first among those who grieve their own sin and who seek repentance and renewal in it.

- That God would grant true revival in your congregation, your community, your denomination, and across the world.

Praying for Suffering, Persecution, & Mourning

"I have told you these things, so that in me you may have peace. In this world you will have trouble. But take heart! I have overcome the world."

–John 16:33

Everyone suffers; everyone hurts. It isn't a question of "if" we will face suffering, persecution, and mourning– it is a matter simply of "when" we will see them. The clear message of the Bible is that we are to expect it. Jesus said to his disciples words that also apply to all believers today: "In this world you will have trouble."[66]

BIBLICAL BASIS

There are two reasons for this, essentially. The first is that the sin of mankind– introduced by the sin of Adam, and perpetuated by all of mankind since then– introduced into our world a fallen

---

[66] John 16:33; note also the comfort given in the rest of the verse: "But take heart! I have overcome the world."

condition of brokenness, decay, and death.[67] While Christ came to redeem us from that fallenness and death, we nevertheless live in a tension of the already present reality of that redemption, and the fulfillment and consummation of it which is not yet complete.

The second reason is that Christ Himself suffered, was persecuted, mourned, and died. We, who are being conformed into Christ's likeness,[68] should expect to also face all of these in order that we might be increasingly perfected into His image. As Christ's suffering was for the purpose of redeeming ours, likewise through our suffering we are brought closer to Him in our redemption.

It is because of this, however, that we need not despair in our pain. While our struggles and trials may be difficult to face, we need not be defeated by them.[69] Though our grief may feel almost like death itself, we do not grieve in a hopeless manner.[70]

---

[67] Romans 5:12 "Therefore, just as sin entered the world through one man, and death through sin, and in this way death came to all men, because all sinned"

[68] Romans 8:29 "For those God foreknew he also predestined to be conformed to the likeness of his Son, that he might be the firstborn among many brothers."

[69] II Corinthians 4:7 "For who makes you different from anyone else? What do you have that you did not receive? And if you did receive it, why do you boast as though you did not?"

[70] I Thessalonians 4:13 "Brothers, we do not want you to be ignorant about those who fall asleep, or to grieve like the rest of men, who have no hope."

Instead, we can see our suffering as a means by which God is making us complete and perfect for His glory, as James, the brother of Christ, said:

> "Consider it pure joy, my brothers, whenever you face trials of many kinds, because you know that the testing of your faith develops perseverance. Perseverance must finish its work so that you may be mature and complete, not lacking anything."[71]

FOUNDATIONS OF PRAYER

Therefore, when we pray for the church about suffering, pain, and struggle, we ought to pray for the completion of God's people in it. Pray that He will develop perseverance and maturity. Pray that He will grant compassion for others through it, and that the cross would increase through it.

Further: consider your congregation. There are people hurting there. Some are facing the sting of very recent events— a death, a sick relative or friend, difficulty at home or at work. Others are nursing wounds long-ago inflicted. Some suffer openly, while others hurt in secret. Some find their faith increased through God's faithfulness to them in suffering; others have begun to doubt and question. Do you pray for these? Pray that your congregation would be present with them in their pain, and that they would not feel alone. Pray that God would heal them of their wounds through the ministry of fellowship. Pray that He would give them hope through the

---

[71] James 1:2-4.

truths taught in His Word, and that He would make His grace real to them through the administration of the Sacraments.

Perhaps you are hurting. How might you pray for your church about your own pain? That they would understand— or if they cannot understand, that they would earnestly believe and accept your pain. Pray that you would experience the nearness of God through them, and that He would bring healing through their love for you.

Realize, also, that there are entire congregations that are in pain. The tragic loss of a pastor, division among the leadership, or a community-wide catastrophe may have led to it. Perhaps the suffering came from within the congregation, or maybe it originated outside of it. There are times when entire congregations need healing. You can pray for these, too: for God to raise up a leader (or a group of them) to tend and shepherd the flock through their healing. For their sister congregations, be they in the community or in a denomination, to come alongside them for encouragement and strength. For unity in the face of this adversity.

Our leaders, of course, need our prayers here. The very nature of leadership in the church often leads to pain: leaders are closer to the pain of others than most, and they share in it more deeply than many. They are prey for spiritual attack, as Satan will often use suffering to test and tempt.[72] Pray for their protection from attack, and that the duties and commitments to leadership would not become imbalanced in their lives so that their families are put to trial. Nevertheless, pray for their faithful, hopeful response to the suffering that they do face, that they may be more perfect and therefore be more perfect ministers to those they lead. Pray for their capacity for suffering to be increased as they share in the burdens of the flock.

We would be remiss, too, if we didn't also pray for the persecuted church. So many of us live in ease when it comes to our freedom to worship as we wish, that it is easy to forget to pray for our brothers and sisters, and our sister congregations, that are actively persecuted for their faith and for the practice of their faith. Pray that God would give them perseverance and endurance in their persecution. Pray that He would glorify Himself through it, that His church would increase in its witness to the gospel. Pray that those who are persecuted would know the comfort of the Holy Spirit, even as they face very real discomfort, and that God would perfect them in their faith through it. And pray that the persecution of the church would come to an end.

---

[72] Job 1:9-11 "'Does Job fear God for nothing?' Satan replied. 'Have you not put a hedge around him and his household and everything he has? You have blessed the work of his hands, so that his flocks and herds are spread throughout the land. But stretch out your hand and strike everything he has, and he will surely curse you to your face.'" (See also Luke 4:9-12.)

PRAYER SUMMARY

- ✦ That God would use suffering to a glorified end, and that those who suffer would know that it is not in vain, but that He is perfecting them through it.

- ✦ For you, and your congregation, to be more present in the suffering of others around them, attentive to their hurting, and that God would use you as an instrument of encouragement and strength.

- ✦ For others in your congregation to recognize and understand your pain, and to love you well in and through it.

- ✦ For your congregation, and/or other congregations, who are hurting as communities— that Christ would tend and shepherd through able leadership, and that He might use other congregations also to encourage and support.

- ✦ That the leadership of your congregation would be prepared to shepherd and care for those in pain, protected from spiritual attack, and increased in capacity for burden-bearing.

- ✦ For the Lord's work in the persecuted church: that those who face persecution would persevere; that their suffering would be a witness to the Gospel; and that they would be relieved of their persecution.

Praying for the Pastor(s) & Officers

"From Miletus, Paul sent to Ephesus for the elders of the church. When they arrived, he said to them: '...Keep watch over yourselves and all the flock of which the Holy Spirit has made you overseers. Be shepherds of the church of God, which he bought with his own blood... Now I commit you to God and to the word of his grace, which can build you up and give you an inheritance among all those who are sanctified.'"

–Acts 20:17-18,28, 32

The leadership of God's people always take a prominent place in Scripture; this is, in part, because they played such a central role in much of the history there. But it is also because God cherishes His leaders, and longs to see their ministries thrive and grow. From Abraham to Joseph, Moses to Joshua, Samuel to David to Solomon, the prophets, the disciples/apostles, and the faithful raised up by them (such as Timothy, Apollos, John Mark, Silas...) — God sets before His people mere men that He has ordained, in all of their failures and brokenness, to lead His people. He has chosen to use leaders in peculiar and grand ways in His church, and He is committed to them.

This is why we have so frequently discussed how we might pray for our leaders throughout this little book. What, you may ask, is left to pray for?

BIBLICAL BASIS

There is yet a great deal to pray for— and if we are committed to pray for God's church, then we must be committed to pray for her leaders. We must, as Paul said in Acts 20, "commit [them] to God and to the word of His grace, which can build [them] up and give [them] an inheritance among all those who are sanctified."[73]

FOUNDATIONS OF PRAYER

What shall we pray for our leaders? How shall we commit them to God?

We might pray first that God would have prepared them, and would continue to prepare them, to be leaders in His church. God has brought them a long way down the path of faith to become leaders, and He will faithfully use their experiences as preparation for His service. This is perhaps especially true in their brokenness: part of the perfection and completion that He is bringing about through brokenness is for the purpose of using them for leadership in His church. Pray that this would be effective, and that the leaders of your congregation— and those of other congregations— would willingly

---

[73] Acts 20:32

draw on their lives, good and bad, for the equipping for leadership that God has given them.

We should pray that they would be effective in leading in the areas God has called them to. This also implies that their sense of calling is clear, and that the unique fitness He has given them for particular aspects of leadership in the church is evident to them. Pray for this as well, as the Lord will often expand or even redirect His saints toward new and better avenues for service that He has for them.

Pray also that He would give them diligence, while protecting them from over-attention and burnout; that He would teach them self-denial and selflessness; that He would protect their families and their marriage, if they are married with children; and that He would cause them to daily submit to Him. Pray that their personal devotional lives would be healthy and thriving: that He would make them into men (and women) of prayer, and devoted to the Word. Pray that they would be willing and able to fulfill the commitments in their lives faithfully, or to forego those commitments they cannot fulfill.

Finally, pray for God to continue to raise up new leaders. The church has a shortage of faithful pastors, and the field of qualified candidates for Elder and Deacon is barren. Pray that your local congregation, as well as the broader church, would attend to the necessity of developing men with leadership potential, discipling and training them toward faithful service. Pray that men would answer the call into leadership and ministry when they hear it. Pray that God would continue to grow His church through godly leadership.

PRAYER SUMMARY

+ That Christ would prepare our leaders to effectively lead His church with humility and wisdom.

+ For our leaders to be faithful to their callings, and that God would continually perfect their sense of calling.

+ That they would be diligent to their work as leaders, healthy in their spiritual and family lives, and committed to faithful obedience to Christ.

+ For the Lord to continue to raise up new leaders your congregation, as well as in other congregations and the larger church.

Praying for Christ's Return

"He who testifies to these things says, 'Yes, I am coming soon.' Amen. Come, Lord Jesus."
—Revelation 22:20

In the time of the New Testament church, there was a sense of anticipation, a longing and hope that Christ would return soon and very soon. In those times, one's expectation in looking for the return of Christ would have been a measure of belief, of sorts: someone who did not frequently and actively long and pray for the return of Christ might have been questioned about whether they truly believed in Jesus with saving faith.

BIBLICAL BASIS

Upon reading the description of what Christ's return will bring in Revelation, one can understand why:

> "Then I saw a new heaven and a new earth, for the first heaven and the first earth had passed away, and there was no longer any sea. I saw the Holy City, the new Jerusalem, coming down out of heaven from God,

prepared as a bride beautifully dressed for her husband. And I heard a loud voice from the throne saying, 'Now the dwelling of God is with men, and he will live with them. They will be his people, and God himself will be with them and be their God. He will wipe every tear from their eyes. There will be no more death or mourning or crying or pain, for the old order of things has passed away.'

He who was seated on the throne said, 'I am making everything new!' Then he said, 'Write this down, for these words are trustworthy and true.'

He said to me: 'It is done. I am the Alpha and the Omega, the Beginning and the End. To him who is thirsty I will give to drink without cost from the spring of the water of life. He who overcomes will inherit all this, and I will be his God and he will be my son.'"[74]

A time when we will live in complete intimacy with God, with death, mourning, crying, and pain done away with— that is something worth longing for! It is truly something to pray and hope will occur soon.

Sadly, as more generations pass since that New Testament church, the saints of God have prayed, longed, and expected the return of Christ less and less. This isn't unique to our day; even in the New Testament era, there were misunderstandings about Christ's return— both letters to the Thessalonians were written to correct such misunderstandings!

---

[74] Revelation 21:1-7

Nevertheless, we must re-learn how to pray for Christ's return. This would be the first task of prayer for the church: that our prayers would regularly include pleas for His return; that our worship, preaching, and fellowship together— indeed, that all of the life of the church might include a sense of anticipation for Christ's return. We must pray that the church of Christ would regain a longing for Christ.

We should pray for our leaders in this way, of course: that they would encourage and redirect our attention toward the hope of what is to come, the consummation of all of the realities made possible through Christ. In times of want, contentment, grief, pain, or delight, such reminders and teaching strengthen us for whatever is before us. Pray that your congregation's leaders would be faithful and diligent in instructing and building up the Body through the right teaching of Christ's return.

Let us pray also for the broader church, that the proper priority of longing for Christ's return would return to prominence. We should pray, also, for protection: emphasis on the return of Christ can become over-emphasis, which often tends to undermine commitment to the ongoing work of the church. Pray that the church would be both expectant and patient, and that we would learn how to keep that balance.

We must not forget to pray for the return of Christ! Certainly, one of the best ways that we can pray for the church— our local congregation and the church universal— is to pray for His soon return. Pray, as the apostle John did, that He would come quickly.

PRAYER SUMMARY

+ That your heart, and the heart of others in your congregation, would be burdened to pray diligently for Christ's return with longing and anticipation.
+ For the leaders of the church to model both longing and anticipation with regard to Christ's coming, and to instruct the body faithfully in a right understanding of it.
+ That the broader church would appropriately prioritize the return of Christ, embodying both expectation and patience.
+ For Christ's soon return in glory.

Appendix: Recommended Reading

The following books are wonderful resources for learning to pray.

+ Jerram Barrs. *The Heart of Prayer: What Jesus Teaches Us*. Published by P&R Publishing, 2008.

+ Arthur Bennett, ed. *The Valley of Vision: A Collection of Puritan Prayers and Devotions*. Published by Banner of Truth Trust, 2002.

+ Kenneth Boa. *Face to Face, volume one: Praying the Scriptures for Intimate Worship*. Published by Zondervan, 1997.

+ Kenneth Boa. *Face to Face, volume two: Praying the Scriptures for Spiritual Growth*. Published by Zondervan, 1997.

+ D. A. Carson. *A Call to Spiritual Reformation: Priorities from Paul and His Prayers*. Published by Baker Academic, 1992.

+ Bryan Chapell. *Praying Backwards: Transform Your Prayer Life by Beginning in Jesus' Name*. Published by Baker Books, 2005.

+ Ole Hallesby. *Prayer*. Published by Augsburg Fortress, 1994.

+ Matthew Henry. *A Method for Prayer: Freedom in the Face of God*. Published by Christian Focus, 1994.

✦ Martin Luther (Archie Parrish, ed.) *A Simple Way to Pray*. Published by Serve International, 2003.

✦ Paul E. Miller, *A Praying Life*. Published by NavPress, 2009.

✦ Andrew Murray. *With Christ in the School of Prayer*. Published by Wilder Publications, 2008.

✦ Eugene H. Peterson. *Answering God: The Psalms as Tools for Prayer*. Published by HarperOne, 1991.

✦ Richard L. Pratt, Jr. *Pray with Your Eyes Open*. Published by P&R Publishing, 1999.

✦ Philip Graham Ryken. *When You Pray: Making the Lord's Prayer Your Own*. Published by P&R Publishing, 2006.

✦ J.C. Ryle. *A Call to Prayer: An Urgent Plea to Enter into the Secret Place*. Published by Audubon Press, 2002.

✦ Edith Schaeffer. *The Life of Prayer*. Published by Crossway, 1992.

Acknowledgements

"I thank my God every time I remember you. "
–Philippians 1:3

I would not have dared to attempt to write this book had it not been for the prompting of the Women in the Church (WIC) ministry of my congregation at Hickory Withe Presbyterian Church (PCA), and especially Jane Mitchell, who was President of the WIC at that time. Thank you, ladies of HWPC!

Many others served as readers and gave valued input about what would become the final version: Richard Burguet, Lou and Nancy Cardamone, Phil Douglass, Ann Louise Eubanks, Lee Ferguson, Dana Perkins, David Stewart, Dave Schmitt, and Adam Tisdale. Many thanks to all of you for your service.

Naturally, my wife Marcie, who is my favorite companion and my heart's true friend, was a great support and encouragement to me throughout the writing; she served me, and this book, with enduring patience and love as she read, re-read, proofread, and discussed the manuscript with me at length. Thank you, Marcie, for your love for me and for my writing; I am grateful to God for you.

Above all, to Christ be all praise and glory for whatever value this humble work might be to His Bride and His Kingdom.

About the Author

Rev. John Edgar Eubanks, Jr. was born in Columbia, South Carolina, in 1972. He received a Bachelor of Arts from the University of South Carolina, and a Master of Divinity from Covenant Theological Seminary. Ordained in the Presbyterian Church in America (PCA), Rev. Eubanks serves a congregation in Eads, Tennessee. Ed also serves as the Co-Director of Doulos Resources. Ed and his wife Marcie have four children.

Ed has been writing for publication since 1998, and has also published the *Covenant Discipleship* Communicants' Curriculum, which he co-authored with Richard L. Burguet; an updated edition of James M. Chaney's *William the Baptist* (of which Ed was the editor); both of these titles are available through Doulos Resources. Ed has written numerous articles in print and online, as well. For more information about Ed, and to read more of his writing, visit his website: www.edeubanks.com.

About Doulos Resources

Our goal is to provide resources to support the church and kingdom, and to build up and encourage the pastors and leaders within the church. Our resources follow the model of Ephesians 4:12– "to prepare God's people for works of service, so that the body of Christ may be built up." We produce books, curricula, and other media resources; conduct research to advance our goals; and offer advice, counsel, and consultation. We are Reformed and Presbyterian, but not exclusively so; while we do not lay aside our theological convictions, we believe our resources may be useful across a broader theological and ecclesiastical spectrum.

Our goal with *For All the Saints*, as with all of our resources, is to offer well-edited, high-quality, and useful materials at an affordable price that makes our resources accessible to congregations and members of the church.

If you are interested in ordering additional copies of *For All the Saints*, or to order other materials that Doulos Resources offers, please visit our website: www.doulosresources.org. If you are ordering in quantity for a church or other ministry, contact us to inquire about a discount for quantity orders.

Made in the USA
Charleston, SC
28 May 2011